BEADS TO BUCKSKINS

BY
PEGGY SUE HENRY

Contained in this Volume are a series of never before exposed patterns.
Updated techniques
Larger illustrations to make hard to follow techniques, easier.
New and exciting ways to apply your beading skills to meet today's fashions.

ontents

Introduction

This series of books are intended to inspire and teach people about beadwork and buckskin garments. How to create patterns and stimulate your own creative ability. Making it possible for everybody to get involved, regardless of nationality or country you live in. Beadwork is loved the world over.

If you see something you like within these pages, try making one like it for yourself. That's a wonderful compliment to the original designer. And what better way to learn. Lots of people have begun that way. My point is: It does not take any credit away from you or the original designer to make a piece of beadwork that has already been done before. 1 have stated in other volumes that "there is really nothing new in beadwork that hasn't been done before, but just revised". Patterns vary, colors change, but the techniques remain the same. Combining techniques in one project will give a different and exciting look. An array of breathtaking designs come from nature. The flowers growing in your front yard or birds nesting. Wild animal photographs and almost any object that is photographed can be transposed to beadwork.

Securing traditional styles and preserving some of the Native American techniques, is part of this Authors objectives. However, not all beadwork exposed through this series deals with the indian traditions. We try to cover as many types and styles as possible by giving photo coverage of beaders all over the world. The contemporary projects exposed throughout this series are elaborately done and the extraordinary skills of the people who created them is almost overwhelming. You too, can learn how to master the beads and create professional designs by using the techniques illustrated in this series. You will find step by step instructions to guide you through every detail. There is a lot more to beading then just big, impressive beaded garments. You will find projects of all different sizes from earrings to purses. Quick, fun and very easy to do. I'm sure you will enjoy beading. Become an achiever and begin this exciting hobby.

We at Beads to Buckskins Publications are here to help you in any way we can. All questions must be by mail and a self-addressed stamped envelope enclosed for reply. No phone calls please.

Acknowledgements

Because we are endeavoring in new avenues concerning the series, I would like to thank my secretary, Denise Babcock for all her help, support and patience in producing this volume.

I could not do this alone. There are some very important people I would like to thank for all their encouragement from phone calls and letters to our company. I have received thousands of letters from beaders and leather craft people all over the world, expressing their gratitude and offering to share their beadwork accomplishments with us. So to all of you, I send my heartfelt **Thank You.** A special thanks goes out to my friends, Sue St. Martin, Kay Fielding, Melody Abbott, Susan Claxton, Doris Barnes, Mary Rowley, Frieda Bates, Erma Koemghsburg, Joyce O'Quinn, the Wendy Mesa Store in Gallup, New Mexico, (owner Beverly Morgan), Jennifer Tallbear, Alice Hardie of Hardies Crafts in Quartzsite, Arizona, Ella Johnson-Bentley, Simone, of Little Eagle Trading Post in Palm Beach, Florida, and many others who have shared their beadwork in photo with me. I appreciate all the hard work and dedication you contribute to your craft.

The instructional illustrations and patterns in this volume were done by the Author. As for the patterns used by the beaders in the photo sections of this and all volumes of "Beads to Buckskins", I can not be responsible. Their original origin is not known to me and my only interest is showing the finished products of beadwork of other people not publishing the pattern of that particular beadwork.

There are other techniques not shown in this volume that have been illustrated in the first six volumes: loom beading, split loom necklace illustrations, overlay or applique stitch, edge or fret stitching, lazy stitch, brick-stitch earring techniques and pattern, spanish lace earings, cradle board earrings, peyote stitch, daisy chain and indian flower along with the chevron technique, moccasin and buckskin shirt and squaw dress, peyote stitch (new method), beaded belt buckles, hair ornaments, brain tanning method, loom beading without-a-loom, cabochon jewelry instructions, beaded fringe, "best kept secrets" off-loom weaving, quill work, tambour beading, tribal color identity, navajo loose weave necklace and earring techniques. **And in this volume, never before exposed patterns, updated techniques made easi-**

er, and new and exciting ways to apply your beading skills to meet today's fashions. In all of the above subjects, have been illustrated with instructions in Volumes One, Two, Three, Four, Five and Six. Add to it the patterns in this volume and you have over fourteen hundred and fifty patterns to choose from, along with some new techniques in each volume. I have tried to make learning beading as easy as possible.

I would like to thank God for my wonderfully, supportive husband, Richard Henry. He has given me the inspiration and the desire to continue on with this project.

The Native American has contributed a tradition to beadwork and I'm very proud of my Indian Heritage. But I'm especially proud of my Navajo mother, Heneretta Bedonie of Flagstaff, Arizona. This gentle lady never tires of being what she is; first mother, then an advisor, next my inspiration. She continually gives her all to me. Thanks Mom.

A big, giant step has been taken and a special thanks to Chad Rudder of Radio Shack/Tandy Corporation and Phil Emery of Johnson Printing Company for their professional help in the purchase and installation of our new computer and desk top publishing equipment. We couldn't have done it without both of you.

There is a special person who has worked very closely with me in editing and printing this series of books for the past three years. I have always been able to depend on her never failing dedication to her job and she deserves recognition. So, I thank you Ann Curtis of Johnson Printing for all you've done for me.

I would like to mention that we do have a store source list and a price list available to help with finding beads and beading supplies from areas all over the United States. I have personally picked these stores to help you find the best possible supplies for your craft. The wooden loom illustrated in the first three volumes, the big eye needle mentioned in Volume Five, and the Tambour Needle illustrated in Volume Six, is available through the publishers address on the back. We would certainly be more than happy to send you a copy of the store source list and the price list with the prices of the items mentioned above and much more if you will send a self-addressed stamped envelope to the address on the back of this book with a note requesting it.

About the Author

I truly enjoy all types of crafts. Quilting is a great hobby and leather crafts are fun. Stained glass is beautiful. There are wonderful projects done in wood. Silversmithing is creative. Crocheting, knitting and embroidering are very interesting. Pottery and basket weaving, I haven't challenged yet. I admire and really appreciate all the crafts mentioned, however, my first love is beading. Pure pleasure without guilt, comes from being able to create an elegant necklace and earrings from those tiny little glass donuts of lovely colors. Beads are like paints. You can mix them to create spring, summer, fall, and winter. The only challenge is trying to decide what pattern you would like to create first. After I start and finish a project, I can't seem to stop. I anxiously want to start the next pattern. I find beading has served as a wonderful therapy for relaxing while being profitable at the same time.

The response from other beaders the world over seems to be in complete harmony with my conception on beading. It is like a good book. You can't put it down until finished.

Throughout this series of books, I have tried to share my enthusiasm hoping you too can discover this enchanting craft for yourself.

Some of you reply "easier said than done", but if you have never tried, then you have denied yourself the satisfaction of ever knowing your capabilities. Whatever you love, pick something you really want to learn or a technique you want to accomplish. Tell yourself you can do it, instead of being negative and just begin. I have learned that taking my time and thinking a step or move out, before I take it, actually saves time in the long run and you register it correctly in your mind first. Speed comes with practice. Pride comes with accomplishment. You benefit yourself by becoming an achiever.

I have experienced all negative things that you can apply to yourself, but when I began to think positive, things fell into place. Years ago, I decided I could do beadwork like my grandmother. Soon, I surpassed all my expectations. Now, I'm the grandmother and still expanding my knowledge by developing new look in beading. Arranging colors and designing patterns are fun. Mixing techniques in the same project is wildly creative, more commonly known as contemporary.

In the first six volumes of this series, I have illustrated many techniques and hundreds of patterns. Whether you are a beginner or expert beader, you will find colorful new designs and ideas to suite your fancy.

Early in my career as a costume designer, I realized the potential that beaded leather garments could attain in the fashion industry. So often, people would ask me to teach them how to cut and lace leather. Then, they would always want the added touch of beadwork to finish it off.

Teaching a beading class takes a great deal of preparation and time. During those years of my very busy life, I just couldn't find the time. However, I did promise to write books after I retired and reveal some of the knowledge I have obtained concerning leather, fur, and beadwork.

Most of the basics were passed down to me from my grandmother and mother, but I have added a lot of "learning by trial and error". Perseverance paid off in the long run. Ground work and practical thinking plays a large part in being able to design beadwork. Then, you just have to apply yourself and think positive.

The popularity of wearing a fur in the United States has dropped drastically during the last decade. However, beaded leather garments are still very popular and in demand. I feel that leather and beadwork have become so much a part of the American way of life, it would take a lot to uproot it. Wiping a tradition away that has existed since the beginning of mankind would be like changing history.

There has been some questions about my exposure of the pull thread technique illustrated in Volume #5. One is the origin of my knowledge of it. I don't mind telling you how and where I learned it.

Some of the Navajo rug weavers have used this technique for generations. I am related to many of these people. The elderly women have passed down the use of beads incorporated with pull thread for as long as I can remember. I am not familiar with other interpretations. Only what has been hands on teaching from my relatives. As for my critics, they should take a refreshing and knowledgeable trip to the Native American Indian Reservation and discover just how talented the Native American's are when it comes to beadwork and weaving crafts.

Contemporary styles are beautiful, but traditional will always hold a special place in society. Not because of its simplicity, but rather the generations of people behind it.

I'm very privileged to be one in a position to share that which God has blessed me with.

I still enjoy receiving letters and photographs from different beaders. I try to show as many photos as possible in each volume. Polaroid photos don't reprint well. We are interested in all forms of beadwork and giving credits for your talent. Be an overcomer and develop your creative ability.

Editor's Notes

In the first half of this series, (volumes one through six) I have explained and illustrated many different techniques. Now you will learn how to put these techniques to work for you.

There are hundreds of ways to use beads to your advantage. In the single capacity of jewelry, there are untold numbers of thousands of dollars earned. Beadwork is not a passing fad. It has remained through centuries and is still growing in popularity. With such a solid repertoire to build your hobby or craft business on, the chances of loosing are minimized.

If you could design the ultimate beading pattern, what techniques would you use? To help inspire your imagination, we have exposed a series of patterns in each volume, with suggestions on arranging colors to spark ideas for creating masterpieces. You can be successful from the moment you decide to take up beading. "Beginning with Basics" to the most complex techniques.

Tradition still controls technique, but design warrants change in some upbeat styles of the nineties and into the twenty-first century. There seems to be a demand for bright splashes of color in contemporary flowing designs with not a lot of exact detail on shapes. More like colorful sound waves for pattern.

It seems the technology of automation overtakes everything as time passes. More and more people are trying to hold on to tradition. One of the few crafts that remains pretty much the same is beadwork. Nothing compares to the art of hand crafted beadwork.

I'd like to mention the Craft Center in Washington D. C. again. The Center serves the interest and needs of low-income artisans by providing technical assistance and information to help artisans achieve markets to sell your crafts. Need help in starting your own business? Looking for sources for low-cost credit? Crafts Center members can receive information on groups, organizations and individuals which provide information in these, and more, crafts areas. Members also receive "Craft News", a quarterly newsletter which is a source of information on crafts activities worldwide, and "Development and Marketing Manual". Membership dues are $35 annually for artisans.

For further information, please write The Craft Center, Membership Director, 1001 Connecticut Ave, N. W., Suite 1138, Washington, D. C. 20036.

In this volume, several appliqued sketches have been transposed from Volumes 5 and 6 to bead graph. It can be done!

Tips For Marketing Your Crafts

There are a lot of programs across the United States for helping to market your crafts. A great way to show your work in your local area is through swap meets and craft shows. "Word of mouth" travels fast.

A buddy system works well for people who can't get away to do shows. A group and each person in the group takes a turn at doing a craft show, selling the work of everybody in the group. Each person shares in the expense, but keeps the profits of his own sales. You have to keep an updated inventory of what you have in stock and prices. If you have twelve people in your group and you do 24 shows a year. Chances are you would only have to do two a year yourself. That leaves the other eleven months for constructing more crafts.

Local community auctions are good for selling crafts. Most are held regularly at the county fairgrounds.

There are thousands of craft stores across the United States that buy and sell beadwork. A good source of information is the "Craft Supply Magazine", Reader Service Center, P. O. Box A-3931, Chicago, Illinois 60690-9990. This magazine prints a yearly directory which is a buyers guide for the professional crafter. It lists hundreds of stores and companies in the craft industry. You will also find where to buy publications that list craft shows throughout the United States.

Keep in mind, the Craft Center in Washington, D. C. (address in Editors Notes of this volume).

Sometimes when people do beadwork or other detailed crafts that take a lot of concentration and time, they go through what is know as a "burn out period", which means you need a break or rest from what you are doing for a few weeks. Then, it's enjoyable when you get back into it. It's these times that you need to be prepared for in your craft business. Don't schedule yourself so busy that your craft skills can't keep up. Once you have established a market and can't keep up and can't meet the quota. The buyer will look elsewhere for merchandise. Sometimes it's best to work with other crafters and they can fill in for you. Or you can buy their crafts to resale.

The craft business is a large industry and in the corner of that industry is beadwork. There just isn't enough beaders to keep up with the market demand in the United States. So, merchants are looking to other countries for manufacturers and most of what they are getting is a cheap imitation, poorly made. There are, however, some nice pieces coming out of Japan, but they are very expensive.

Every technique in beading is worth learning. From the most elaborate to the simplest. Each has its place in the market. Southwestern styles are very much in demand as well as crystal stage costumes and jewelry.

If you make a good piece of beaded jewelry, check with the jewelry stores in your area for selling or consigning for sale on percentage basis. There are a lot of "Trading Posts" and Indian artwork galleries across the country that buy beadwork.

Advertise your craft. Let people know what you do. The response will work in your favor if you persevere. Start a portfolio of your work. Keep it up to date and as colorful and clean looking as possible. Take orders from it . If your don't have a particular piece in stock, give the customer a delivery date, allowing yourself time to make and ship it. Always deliver on time.

There are many craft magazines published monthly. Thumb through them the next time you are at the grocery store. In the back of the magazines you will find a classified section. Occasionally, you will find stores advertising to buy crafts. That's the magazine to buy or subscribe to. One that supplies the information you need.

Again, I suggest you make a good supply of stock before you adventure into wholesaling your crafts. Once the ball starts rolling, it's hard to keep up with. It's also important that, once you establish a price, you can't very well raise or fluctuate them without controversy. So do a little groundwork and check the market price for crafts comparable to your own. If it's compatible, then you can establish your prices accordingly.

I receive phone calls and letters regularly from beaders asking me to price their work for them. I can't do it for many reasons. Mainly, only they know the time and expense in their work. And it's impossible to judge other peoples work sight unseen and I'm not familiar enough with prices across the country myself to generalize a price for any piece of beadwork. So, you will have to develop your own qualifications or pricing. But, don't price yourself out of the market. Repeating business is good business.

The earrings shown in this grouping are done by "Simone" of Little Eagle Trading Post, Palm Beach, Florida. She has incorporated quill work on the outside pieces to create a traditional look.

Here is a close up of the Thunderbird Earrings done by Simone in bold red and gray with accents of white and black.

What a lovely grouping of quill and bead work in this photo by Simone. She has incorporated turquoise, rust, green, black and of course, the natural quills.

Bone pipe beaded choker created by Simone in turquoise, earth tone rusts, and fringed in black leather.

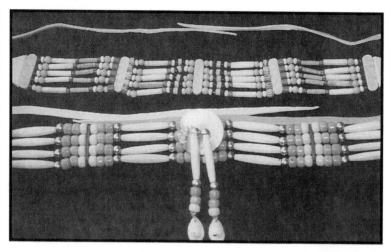

Look at these traditional beaded belts designed by "Simone" of Little Eagle Trading Post, Palm Beach, Florida. The top belt is designed with African Trade beads in naturals, turquoise, brown, earth tones. The bottom belt displays the same colors, but she uses the incorporation of Crow Beads in this design.

Here is a close up of Simone's quill and beaded earrings in reds, yellows, and turquoise.

Joan Lobster of Winnipeg, Manitoba, Canada has created these baby moccasins in a deep midnight blue with the design done in earthtones and various shades of blues.

Kay Fielding has created these earthtone rust colored silk and beaded earrings, "woven on a hoop". The different shades of coordinating beads, intermingled with the hand woven silk, creates a unique design.

Kay Fielding has shared with us her wonderful Silk and Beads Jewelry Creations. Also shown in the color section.

Think about silk threads of beautiful earth tones. Incorporate some beads to match. Spin a weave of silk through the beads, and Kay Fielding came up with this beautiful dream and transformed it to reality as you can see. Also shown in the color section.

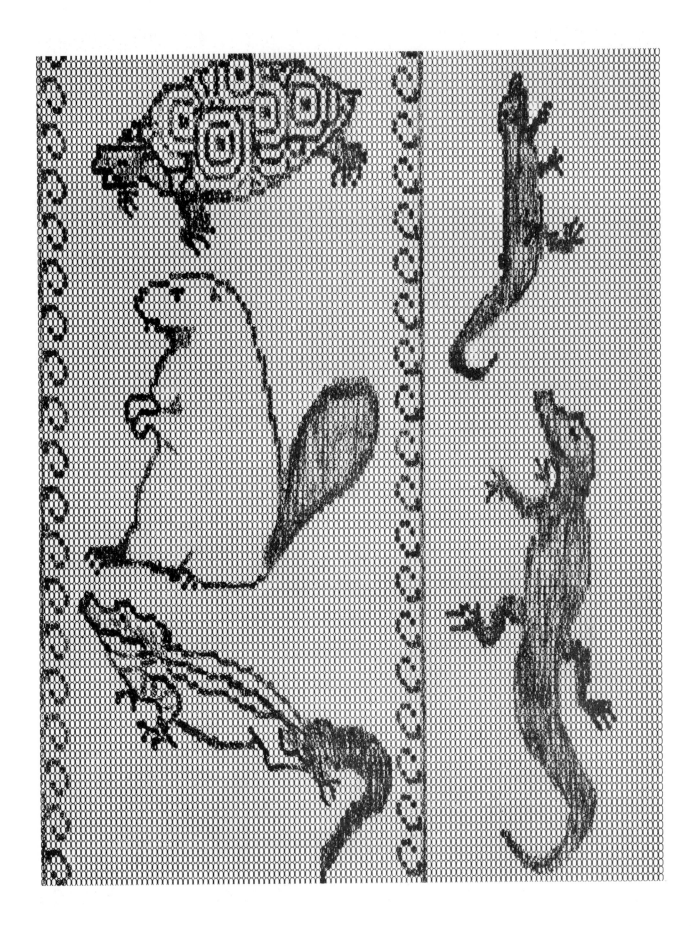

Southwestern History

Understanding the grass roots origin of South Western Indian Art and how their enduring and always popular styles came about is told in America's history.

Before history was recorded in America, there were the Native Americans of the southwest. American history begins with Columbus stumbling upon a new continent in search of a western route to India in 1492--five hundred years ago.

Actually, it began many hundreds and perhaps thousands of years before that historical year of Columbus. One thriving city along the cliffs at Puye Cave dwellings were hallowed into the volcanic tufa in the Canyon of the Rits de Las Frijoles, about 1500 to 1800 years ago. Ruins of the great communal house of the Tyunyi spread like a horseshoe on the floor of Frijoles Canyon. These ruins are a part of Bandelier National Monument.

There are excavated ruins of Pueblo Bonito in Chaco Canyon National Monument. The feet of prehistoric men wore a path in the solid stone at Tsankawi. Ladders led to levels above the ground. In some spots, they left pitagraphic records hundreds of years before Columbus.

The indians have left the history of his civilization in his dwelling places as he deserted them, in the piles of broken pottery of the burial grounds and in the Kivas; sacred council rooms of the clans. Scientists are daily working to solve some of the questions about his origin and reason for abandoning his cliff dwelling and communal villages. There are many theories about the origin of the American Indian. But the fact is, they were the first Americans.

The ceremonial dances and sacred prayers of the modern Native Americans today, still reflects a whisper of the ancient ones. If you watch and listen closely, you can catch a glimpse of long ago history preserved in today's indian, as they continue to preform these ancient customs passed down from who knows how long.

The great age of the prehistoric Southwestern Indian was between 1000 A. D. and 1540 A. D. when their expansion had reached its limit. They reached their highest development as cultivators and artisans, wrestling a living from the soil under adverse conll ditions and creating beautiful objects for daily use. Pottery, baskets, ornaments of bone and turquoise were used in the daily life of these now long dead people.

The indian is a born artist. He

proves this by devoting infinite care to his work, whether it is fashioning a piece of pottery for household use or beating out an intricate bit of jewelry for personal adornment. Time is no object.

The Navajo people are a race apart. There is no other people like them. A visit to their country is a treat no traveler should miss.

Silversmithing and rug weaving are the outstanding arts among the Navajos. The Navajo rug is famous for its workmanship as well as for its durability. The Apaches, fierce marauders of the plains, are adept at weaving baskets and making beaded articals.

Many generations ago the Navajos learned how to weave from their neighbors, the Pueblos. It wasn't long until this amazing tribe was far more skilled then their teachers. Until the Spaniards arrived, both tribes had woven cotton. The Conquistadors introduced sheep into the country and the Navajos became shepherds.

The Navajo Woman never follows a pattern in weaving. She makes up her pattern as she weaves, which is the reason no two Navajo rugs are exactly alike. Most follow geometric lines, but the colors are so harmonized that one is hardly conscious of the angular lines which compose the figures in the patterns. Black, red, and gray are found in most rugs. Vegetable dyes are frequently used.

Pottery-making among the Pueblos have grown into an industry which each year markets thousands of pieces to the world outside their culture.

Pottery-making came about as a result of necessity. The indian needed vessels for storage of food, water, and cooking utensils. The women learned how to fashion by hand the beautiful bowls. Many were decorated with paints made by grinding various colored stones. Yucca Fiber was used for brushes. The decorations usually consist of geometric or conventionalized animal and bird designs.

When people refer to southwestern artifacts, they are actually recalling past centuries of existence when a proud, stately and magnificent people lived in the southwest. The mysterious disappearance of some may never be understood. It is important that we don't allow anymore of our Native American culture to be swallowed up by modern technology before it can be recorded for the future generations.

Many of the patterns used in this series of have been passed down for centuries. Some are from legend, others from pitagraphic designs on cave or canyon walls. Certain shapes were symbolic to individual nations. Refer to Volume Six for Tribal Identity by color and beadwork.

Kachina.

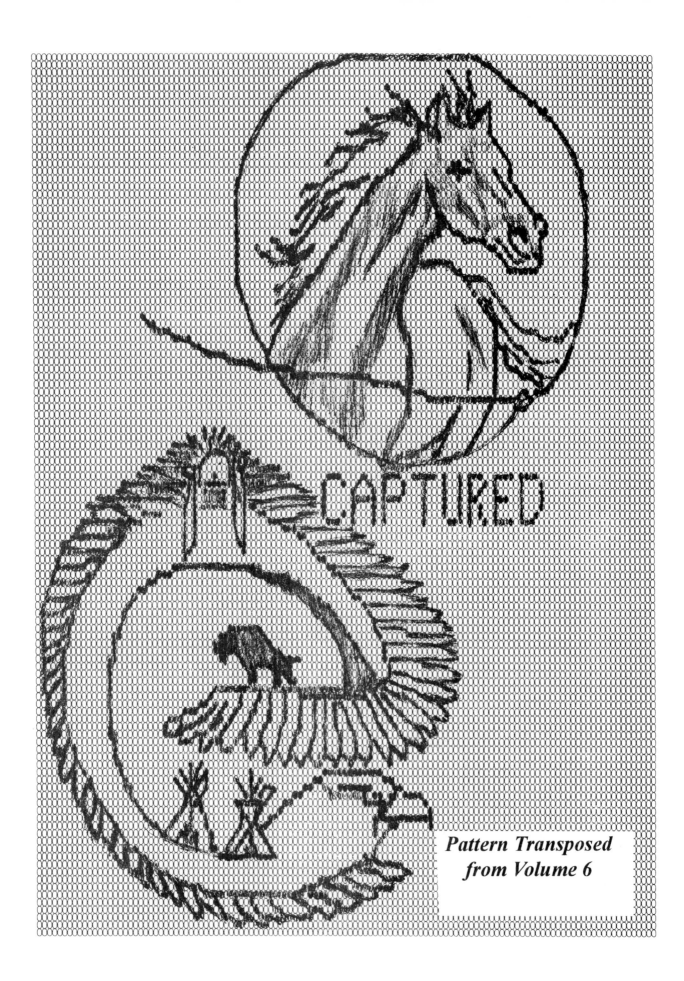

CAPTURED

Pattern Transposed from Volume 6

THE SCOUT

This beaded horn was done by Ella Johnson-Bentley in various earth tones.

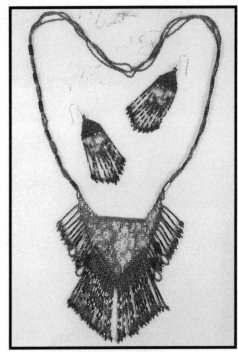

Ella's first loomed piece. Body of design in black lined beads. The rest in hematite with twisted bugles in the fringe.

An original design by Ella. Pansies are inlayed in the center in yellows, blues, purples.

Ella shows pot necklace from pattern in Volume 3, page 25.

Transposing Pictures To Bead Graph

There are some critics who say the sketches in this series can not be used for beading patterns. However, I am convinced that they really haven't put much effort into trying to bead them. A good example of how to use these sketches has been done by Doris Barnes.

In Volume Five, page 9, I show a sketch of Carolina paroquet. Doris enlarged the pattern and arranged the in flight paroquet in the background and applique beaded them for the beautiful purse shown in color on page 70 of Volume Six.

Another example: The eagle sketch on page 56 of Volume Two is shown beaded in color on page thirty-four of Volume Two. Again this sketch has been appliqued.

One of the greatest compliments you can pay to someone is to imitate or try to do what they do. This Author greatly admires Edgar Jackson's work. I was quite taken with Frieda Bates' purse he had done. I show the original purse on page 60 of Volume 2. I would like to have shown the original on the front cover of Volume Three, but my husband insists that the front cover of each book be done by me. An since he is the publisher and president of this company, we have come to that agreement. However, I would like to mention my close friend Sue St. Martin. She has helped me a great deal by doing some of my patterns illustrated in this series in order to show them in the color sections. Sue and I have both retired from country western entertainment and costume designing.

Creating a pattern for beadwork is not as difficult as it appears. It can be done with a sheet of transparent bead graph paper or by tracing the picture onto beadgraph paper.

If you use the tracing method, you will need a bead graph paper printed on tracing paper which can be purchased at Tandy Leather stores or your local craft store that carries beading supplies. You may also send a self-addressed stamped envelope to the address on the back and we will send you a source list with many bead supply and craft stores listed throughout the United States. Some offer catalogs and all will ship mail orders.

Keep in mind as you are tracing the pattern, the geometric formation of the beads prevents capturing many of the smaller detailed lines, such as facial expression, cheek bones and such. However, by using the right colors and blending of beads, you can achieve a depth of shadow detail as in painting. As you progress in beading, you will discover which technique is easier for you. Whether you prefer loom or off-loom weave, the same graphed pattern can be used for both techniques.

When using a transparent film (usually 8 1/2" X 11" in size) tracing isn't necessary. If you have access to a copy machine, simply lay the transparency over the picture and place it face down on the copy machine. The copy machine will print the beadgraph over the picture in black and white. Next, color the graphed pattern in the colors of your choice. If your picture is larger than the transparency, you may want to reduce your picture or copy it in two, overlapping sections.

If you don't use a copy machine, simply tape the transparency in place with clear tape, over the picture. If your picture happens to be in color, then you have saved a lot of time and guess work as to what colors to use. In this volume, I have sketched an indian fishing for applique and transposed him onto graph for loom or off-loom. The composition changes slightly, but can still be identified and when proper bead colors are used the graph detail improves.

For applique beading, you can bead right through the paper pattern. This Author has pieces of beadwork from the late 1800 hundreds that still has parts of the paper pattern under the beads. However, I prefer to trace the pattern onto thin interfacing then attach a more stable material or leather for the backing.

When appliqueing onto a fabric garment, you should always use an interfacing to back with. It will help support the beadwork while keeping the threads from pulling through the fabric.

A quick transposition that works well for me. Again, you will need a copy machine. The cross stitch fabric "aida cloth" is a very stiff material and thin enough to use as paper. I have trimmed aida cloth 14 count, down to page size of this book, pressed all the wrinkles out, made sure there were no frayed edges and hand fed it through my copy machine as copy paper. The picture in the machine copies beautifully onto the aida cloth. Cross stitching with beads is a wonderful technique for making hat bands, belts and garments. You have the backing and pattern all in one, which can easily be attached to leather or fabric.

There are hundreds of cross stitch patterns and books on the market that can be used for beading. Most all have color suggestions. I encourage you to check the book area in your local craft stores and experiment a little. That's the fun of beading. Trying something different.

Once again, Melody Abbott has out done herself with this geometrically designed scabbord. The earth tones and white beads are complemented by the dark leather background and is very appealing.

Melody shows this scabbord of horse head in basic earth tones. Great detail!

Ella Johnson-Bentley of Juneau, Alaska has created her version of the deer pattern shown in Volume One, page 34. She shows hers in turquoise background with accents in earth tones.

Black beaded necklace by Ella Johnson-Bentley with accents of bold reds, yellows, greens, and blues. Part of a pattern, page 22 of Volume Five.

BOBCAT

BIG
HORN

SHEEP

Pattern Transposed from Volume 6

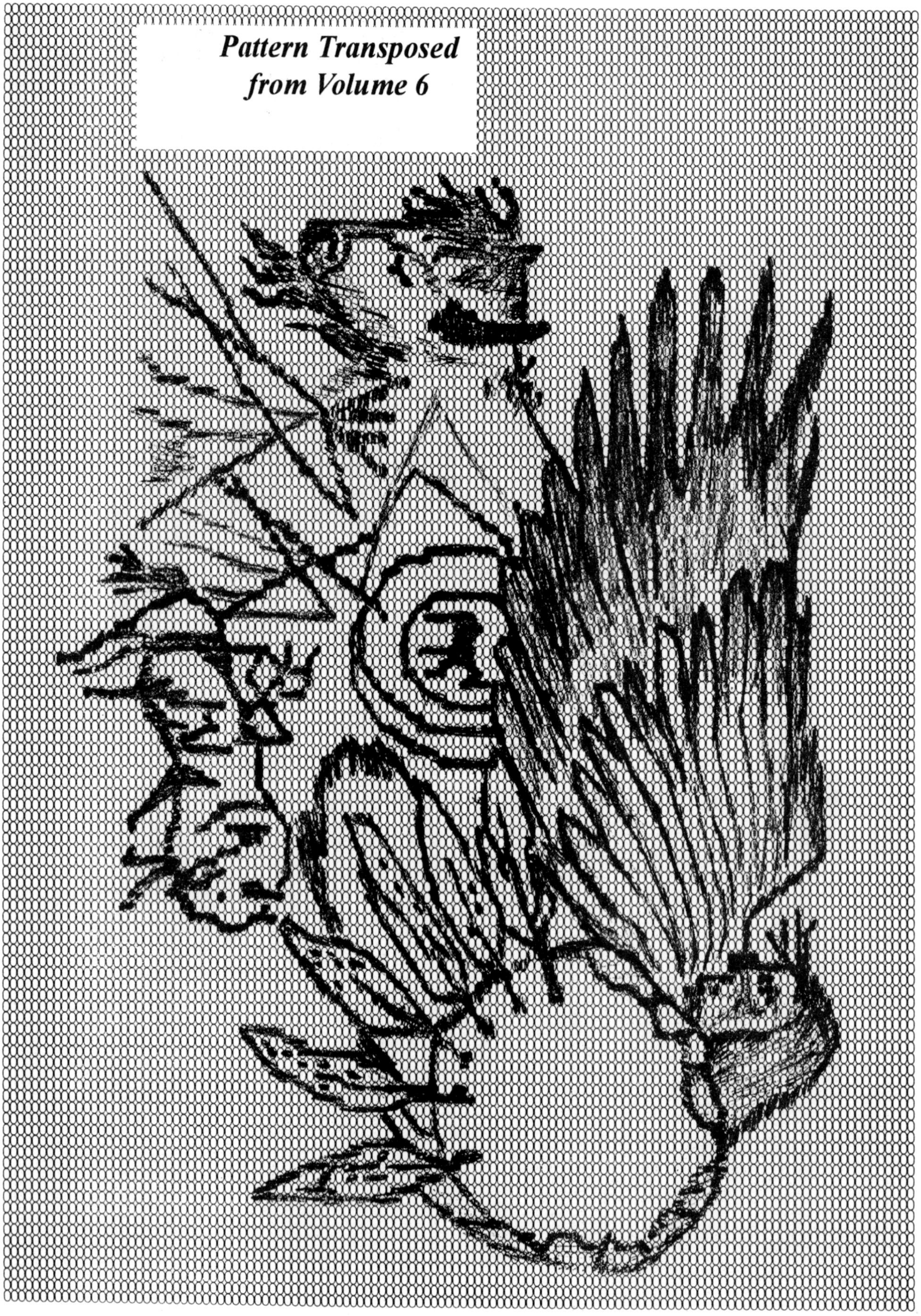

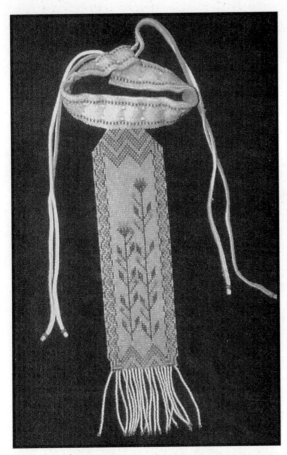

Melody Abbott arranged these lovely soft shades of creams and purples into a gift for the Author. Thank you, Melody.

Something old has been arranged into something new. Using a fossil as a cabochon, Doris Barnes applied beads and Mr. Mell Ball of Quartzsite, Arizona used silver. Both are great!

Susan Claxton has been seeing red in this delicate necklace. Notice bead buttons and loops.

Geometric and fringed. This beauty is done in a pony bead size. Photo courtesy of Wendy Mesa, Gallup, New Mexico.

Pattern Transposed from Volume 5

Pattern Transposed from Volume 5

*Patterns Transposed
from Volume 2*

QUAIL

**Patterns Transposed
from Volume 2**

*Patterns Transposed
from Volume 2*

Authors, Three Tribes designed earrings. Navajo peyote stitched corn earrings. Ojibwa side-stitched earrings and Seneca off-loom eye earrings.

Joyce O'Quin has created these beautiful pinwheel and Spanish Lace earrings.

Kay Fielding created these silk weave, brick-stitched earrings with larger drop beads. Exciting effect!

Susan Claxton has created these peyote stitched earrings and fringed cover in blues, pinks, and whites.

Kay Fielding has woven silk threads and beads on a metal loop for a soft contemporary look.

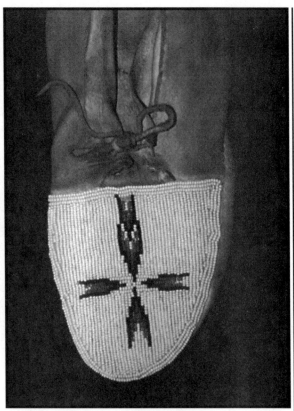

Beaded moccasins have been in author's collections thirty-four years.

Loom-beaded arm bands and belts. Photo courtesy of Wendy Mesa, Gallup, New Mexico.

Red rose pattern on blue background. Belt and hair ornament. Photo courtesy of Wendy Mesa, Gallup, New Mexico.

Kay Fielding has brilliantly used silk and beads to weave this lovely, earth tone necklace.

Kay has used multi-colored silk yarns of soft earth tones with silver and shades of green beads.

Kay exhibits a contemporary dream in beautiful silk yarn woven with beads and ornaments of contem-porary design.

Kay has truly mastered the art of silk weaving as you can see in this split loom necklace.

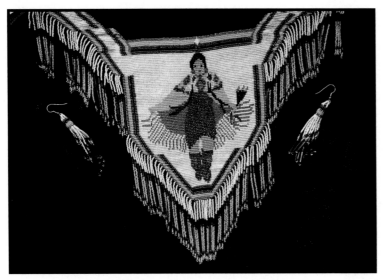

Doris Barnes (Author's sister-in-law) beaded this graceful fancy shawl dancer for the back of her vest. Matching earrings. Size 14/o beads.

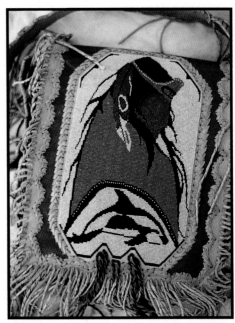

Melody Abbott constructed this Eskimo Maiden with a Killer Whale incorporated at the bottom onto a leather purse. Size 14/o beads.

Mary Rowley beaded this warrior and horse in tiny size 16/o and smaller beads. Great detail, Mary!

Melody shows off her one-of-a-kind talent in this exquisite "Ghost" beaded purse in size 14/o beads.

Beaded Kachina. Photo courtesy of Beverly Morgan, Wendy Mesa Store, Gallup, New Mexico.

My old friend Beverly at Wendy Mesa, Gallup, New Mexico allowed me to photograph this set of Kachinas.

Beaded Kachina, Courtesy of Wendy Mesa, Gallup, New Mexico. Each Kachina on this page is done with pony beads.

Beaded Kachinas done with pony beads. Photo courtesy of Windy Mesa, Gallup, New Mexico.

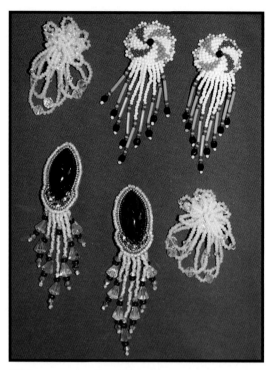

This group of enchanting earrings was also done by Joyce O'Quin.

My "Sister, Friend" Joyce O'Quin created these lovely cabochon earrings as a gift for me. Thank you, Joyce.

Ojibwa side stitch earrings. This unusual technique is time consuming, but well worth it!

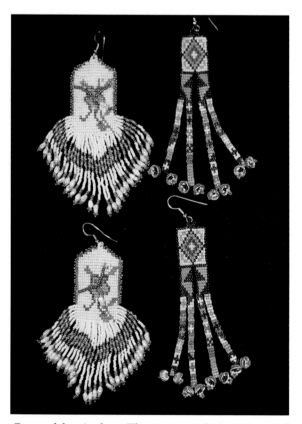

Created by Author. The same technique is used on both pair of earrings. Illustrated this volume. Size 14/o beads.

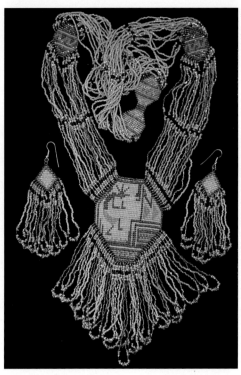

The famed Flute Player done in rose and shades of blue has played and danced his way into many pieces of beadwork. Author.

My friend, Frieda Bates, has created something unique and beautiful in this expanded winged Kachina. Neckline beads are 2mm Heishé. Center size 14/o beads.

This Papago-styled progressive star in size 11/o beads, off-loom weave. Created by Erma Koenigsburg.

Erma Koenigsburg of Liberty, Missouri, learned this off-loom weave from a Papago Indian lady in the 1970s.

This assortment of beaded buckles and hair pieces are primarily done by the Southwestern Indians around Gallup, New Mexico. Courtesy of Wendy Mesa.

Last year, I sent beads and cabochons to Jennifer Tallbear and asked her to make me something pretty and, sure enough, she did.

These colorful peyote beaded containers were on display at Wendy Mesa in Gallup, New Mexico.

Jennifer used black matter bugles, 12/o cut beads with turquoise cabochons and nuggets on this set of brooch and earrings.

Beaded Kachina done with Pony size beads. Courtesy of Wendy Mesa, Gallup, New Mexico.

Antique Medicine Pouch done in size 11/o beads, Lazy Stitched. Photo courtesy of Hardies, Quartzsite, Arizona.

Susan Claxton has incorporated peyote stitched shell fringe to complement the buffalo and pheasant in flight on this piece.

My friend, Alice Hardie, has shared with us these lovely beaded gloves. The fur is beaver. Courtesy of Hardies, Quartzsite, Arizona.

Beaded pipestone pipe and pouch. Courtesy Wendy Mesa, Gallup, New Mexico.

Doris Barnes created two brown buckskin vests with matching buckle and bolos. The Walking Wolf is on vest backs and Wolf heads on front yokes. 12/o cut beads were used for this great effect

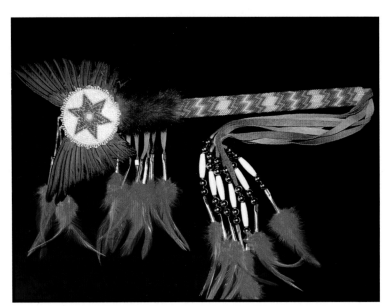

This lovely blue bird fan was presented as a gift to me from my friend, Branda Carl. Beading artist unknown.

Author's husband, Richard, is wearing a black buckskin vest inlaid with antique Indian Woven Rug. A pair of these vests was created by Author.

The Lacy Daisy Weave

This simple, but beautiful technique adds a delicate exciting appearance to any necklace, bracelet, barrett, or belt you decide to use it with. It can be made as wide as you want or as long as you want, and you don't have to worry about stringing a loom or what to do with the end strings, for there are none.

The complex appearance of this weave gives the impression of advanced beading. The simplicity of it can easily be done by a beginner bead-er. Actually it's done in strips, then the strips are connected by the completion of the daisies to create the base strips.

I have illustrated a four bead wide, off loom weave strip with an edge bead attached between every fourth and fifth row. You can make this strip as wide as you wish. You can get a nice leaf pat-tern in a nine bead wide strip, to coor-dinate with the daisy flowers. I have also illustrated how to reduce the width down to two beads wide to give a vine or stem look connecting the daisies. I'm sure once you have tried this tech-nique you will use it often. Each step described is illustrated in the following pages. If you have mastered "Loom Beading Without-A-Loom" in Volume three of this series, then this weave will be an easy series, then this weave will be an easy addition for you. We will begin by making one of the outside

strips. The center strip differs slightly.

Step 1. --Using a single tie, tie a knot bead onto your beading thread about four inches from the end. You will be using this bead later as part of a daisy when you work the end of your thread into your finished beadwork.

Step 2. --String six beads onto your thread. The fifth bead will be part of the daisy, so be sure you choose the color you want the daisy to be. (This bead will be referred to as a daisy bead). Next pass your needle back through the fourth bead, then back through the sixth bead (see Plate #1). Snug the beads gently together. Your daisy bead should be setting on edge between the first and beginning of the second row (See Plate # 2). Continue the row by adding one bead at a time for the next two beads. (Plate # 2)

Step 3. --Each time you begin a row, pick up two beads. Notice the dif-ference when adding a daisy bead. **When adding the edge bead for your daisy flower you pass your needle through the first bead of the last row. (see Plate #1) When not adding an edge bead for your daisy, you pass your needle through the second bead of the last row. (see Plate # 3).**

Step 4. --Since we are making one on the outside edge of the left and right base strips. You are only adding a daisy edge bead to one side, between every fourth and fifth row. (see plate #4)

Don't be concerned about which is left and right. Create them both the same. Then turn one over. Make your strips as long as you want the finished beadwork to be.

Step 5. --The center strip is done exactly as the outside strips with one exception. You must add a daisy edge bead to each side between every fourth and fifth row (see plate #5). Use the same stitch as in step #2 when adding a daisy-edge bead to each side of a row. (see plate # 1) When you have completed the three beaded base strips (the center and both outside edge strips) lay them out flat with the daisy edge beads toward the middle strip. Make sure your strips are the same length.

Step #6 --Tie a knot bead on, four inches from end of thread. This bead will be removed later and the end thread worked back into the beaded strip. Pass your needle through the first row of the outside base strip (see plate #6) Now, you are ready to attach the daisy and connect the beaded strips. Pass your needle through the daisy edge bead and pick up #1 and #2 beads. (see plate # 6) These beads are the petals of the daisy. Now pass your needle through the daisy edge bead on the center strip. Pick up the center bead (#3) of the daisy (you may want to make this bead yellow or orange for the center of the flower) pass your needle

back through the daisy edge bead of the outside base strip. To finish the daisy, pick up beads #4 and #5 (petal beads) and pass your needle back through the daisy edge bead on the center strip. Snug the beads gently together and you have completed the first daisy connection.

Step 7. --Work your needle and thread through the center beaded strip and leave it in position to begin your second daisy (see plate # 6). For the second daisy, reverse the same moves you have done in the first daisy. As you continue creating the daisies, your project begins to take on a lovely lacy appearance. By alternating the colors of each daisy or making each a different color your beadwork takes on a lovely look of spring. Use earth tones for fall flowers.

For a Quick Lacy Daisy Woven Strip

Step 1. Make two; Two bead chains with an edge bead between every fourth and fifth row. (see plate #7).

Step 2. Connect the two bead chains with a daisy, as illustrated in #6 illustration. You can space the daisies one bead longer apart and still get a lacy look (see plate # 9) or you can add an edge bead the full length on the outside strip edge which adds a professional look to your work by covering the strings. (see plate # 10 of Lacy Daisy

Earrings).

This unique little earring is constructed in two parts and is a quickie to make.

Beginning with the top half of the earring for step # 1--Refer to plates # 7 and # 8 of "two bead base strip".

make a two bead strip, omitting the daisy bead, seven beads across. Pass your needle back through the first three beads of row one and back through the fifth and sixth beads of Row Two.

Row Two-- This move leaves your needle in place to begin Row # 3 and you have reduced a bead on the next row.

Row Three--Pick up beads and pass your needle back through the second bead your picked up. Follow the black line of thread arrows as in plate # 13.

The next three beads are attached one bead at a time, completing a five bead row.

Although, row # 4 is only three beads across, you will still have to repeat the same needle position moves as Row 4 and start with a two bead pickup.

The bottom half of the earring begins with a two bead base strip seven beads across (omitting the daisy bead). Next, extend the sides adding the daisy beads as shown in plate # 15. Both sides are the same. You can connect the bottom to the top as you complete each side. Or, if you find it easier to finish the bottom half, complete the daisy as illustrated in plate #6 then con-

nect the bottom to the top, you get the same results either way. Adding fringe is optional, but putting a daisy on the bottom of each fringe is enhancing. For a different earrings you may want to reduce and edge as you go.

This technique makes a lovely earring and is a nice change from the brick stitch. It has lots of options. The little diamond shapes are used on the neckline of necklaces shown throughout this series entitled "Loom Beading With-A-Loom". They can be used in bracelets, on barrettes, or pins. They work well when used for inlaying into leather.

Actually this technique is an extension of the Lacy Daisy Weave. The versatile variation makes it a separate technique when used as an earring. Rows # 1 and # 2 are the same steps illustrated on the edge stitching page plate # 16.

Tie a knot bead on (to be removed later). The first and last beads, you pick up of each row will become part of edge beads shown on the pyramid in plate # 3 of "Reducing and Edging".

Step Two: Beginning the second row. Pick up two beads, (the color of your edge), and pass your needle back through the last bead of the first row. Snug the beads close together. Continue the row attaching one bead at a time. When you complete the second row, add an edge bead between Row # 1 and # 2 as shown in Step # 3 (plate #

18) "Edge Stitching".

For Row Three of the pyramid, you will need to reduce a bead on both sides of the row, as illustrated in Plate # 2 of "Reducing and Edging".

Rows # 4 and # 5 are repeats, using the same moves as Row # 3.

After you have completed the pyramid you can work your needle and thread back through to Row One and add Rows Three, Four, and Five to the the top for a diamond or you can hang fringe across Row One, add a five bead loop to the # 5 Row edge bead for an ear wire connection and you have a beautiful earring with no strings showing.

The two earrings shown on this page have illustrated and written insturctions in this section of the book.

Reducing and Edging Earrings

Pyramid Earring

Diamond Earring

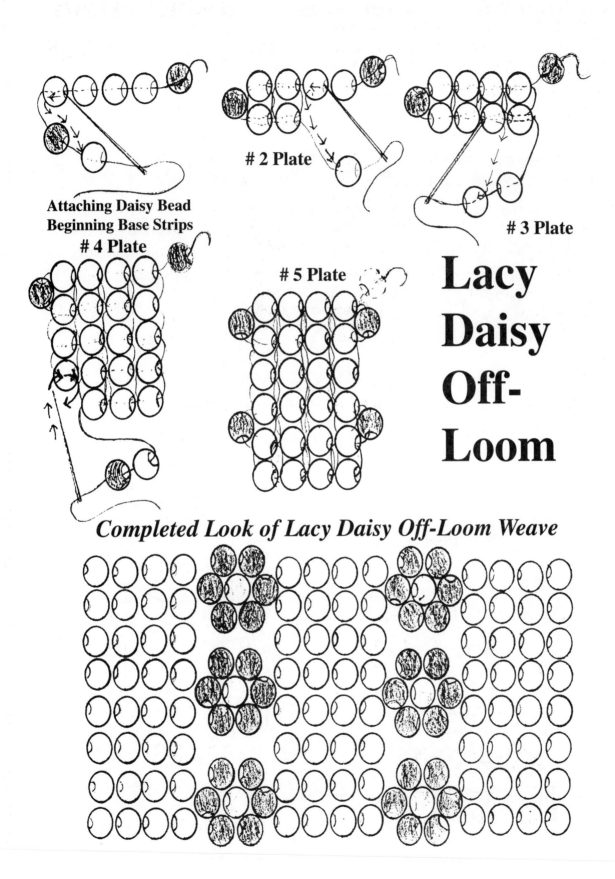

Attaching Daisy Bead
Beginning Base Strips

 # 2 Plate

 # 3 Plate

 # 4 Plate

 # 5 Plate

Lacy Daisy Off-Loom

Completed Look of Lacy Daisy Off-Loom Weave

Connecting Beaded Base Strips with Daisy's

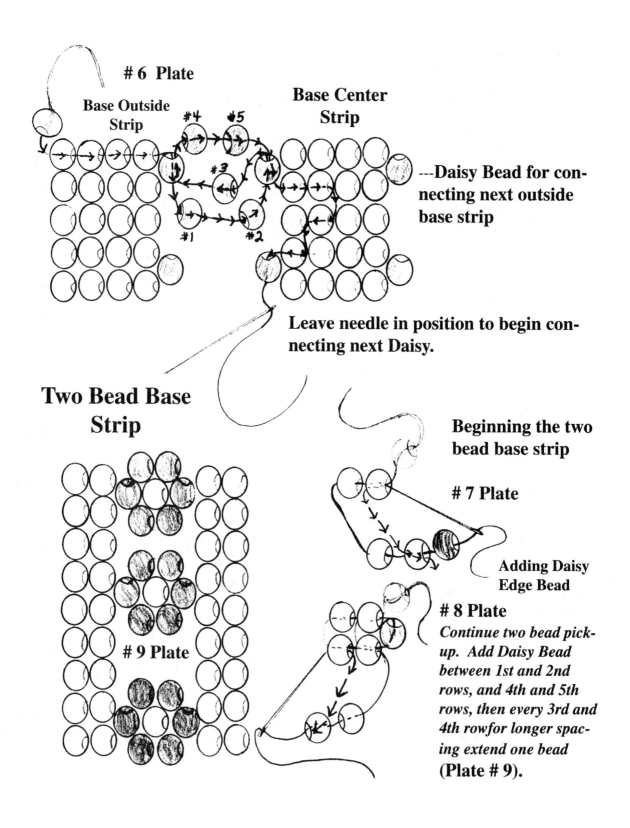

 # 6 Plate

Base Outside Strip

Base Center Strip

#4 #5

#3

#1 #2

---Daisy Bead for connecting next outside base strip

Leave needle in position to begin connecting next Daisy.

Two Bead Base Strip

 # 9 Plate

Beginning the two bead base strip

 # 7 Plate

Adding Daisy Edge Bead

 # 8 Plate
Continue two bead pick-up. Add Daisy Bead between 1st and 2nd rows, and 4th and 5th rows, then every 3rd and 4th rowfor longer spacing extend one bead
(Plate # 9).

Adding a Line of Outside Edge Beads to Base

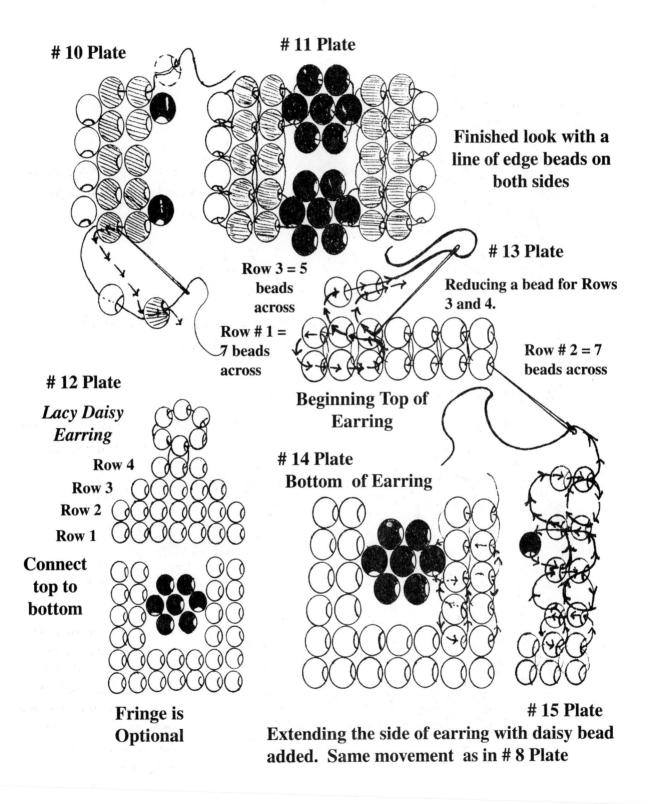

 # 10 Plate

 # 11 Plate

Finished look with a line of edge beads on both sides

 # 13 Plate

Row 3 = 5 beads across

Row # 1 = 7 beads across

Reducing a bead for Rows 3 and 4.

Row # 2 = 7 beads across

 # 12 Plate

Lacy Daisy Earring

Row 4
Row 3
Row 2
Row 1

Connect top to bottom

Beginning Top of Earring

 # 14 Plate
Bottom of Earring

Fringe is Optional

 # 15 Plate

Extending the side of earring with daisy bead added. Same movement as in # 8 Plate

Enlarged Edge Stitching Illustrations
(Each Row as You Go)

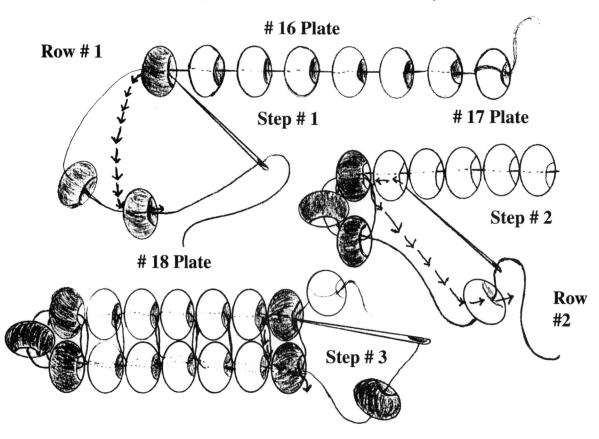

Row # 1

 # 16 Plate

Step # 1

 # 17 Plate

 # 18 Plate

Step # 2

Row #2

Step # 3

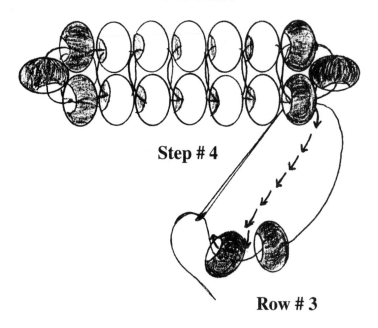

 # 19 Plate

Step # 4

Row # 3

For better understanding, we have done close up illustrations of this stitch

Reducing and Edging

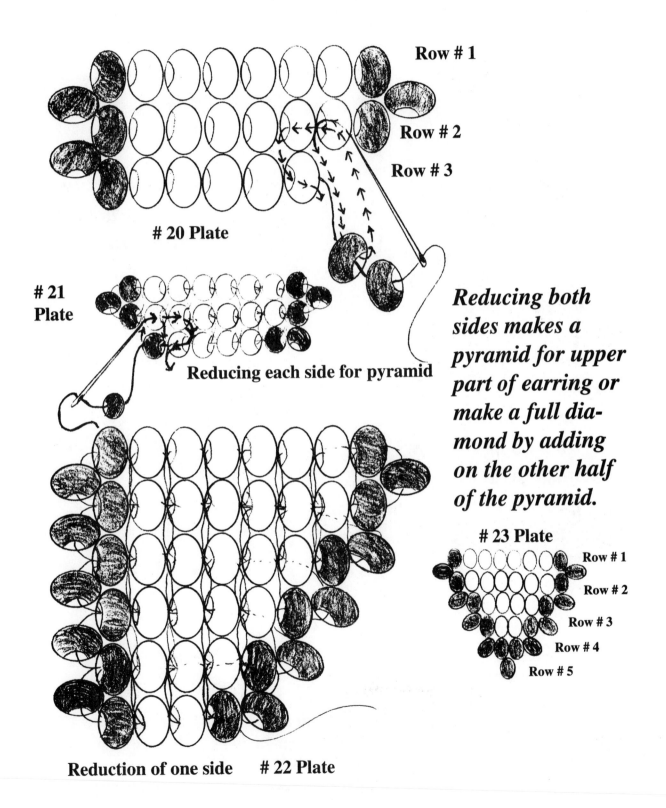

Row # 1

Row # 2

Row # 3

20 Plate

21 Plate

Reducing each side for pyramid

Reducing both sides makes a pyramid for upper part of earring or make a full diamond by adding on the other half of the pyramid.

23 Plate

Row # 1

Row # 2

Row # 3

Row # 4

Row # 5

Reduction of one side   # 22 Plate

Making Looped Earrings

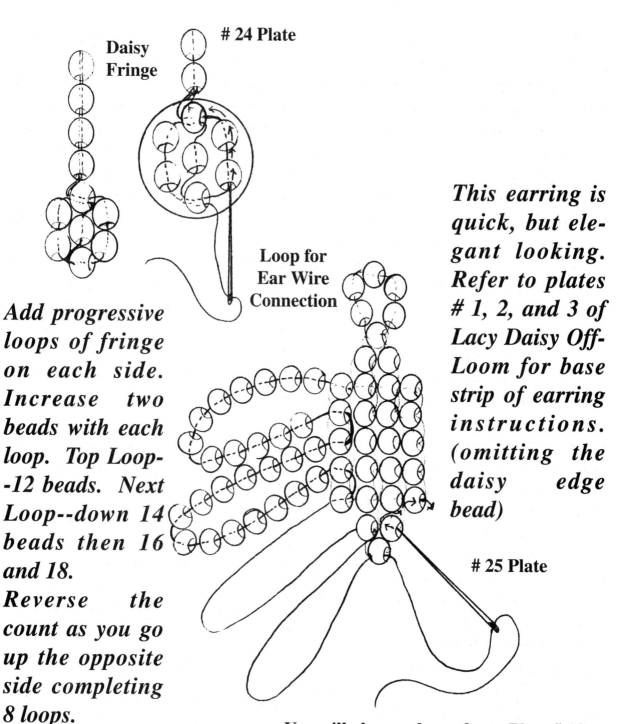

Daisy Fringe

 # 24 Plate

Loop for Ear Wire Connection

This earring is quick, but elegant looking. Refer to plates # 1, 2, and 3 of Lacy Daisy Off-Loom for base strip of earring instructions. (omitting the daisy edge bead)

Add progressive loops of fringe on each side. Increase two beads with each loop. Top Loop--12 beads. Next Loop--down 14 beads then 16 and 18.
Reverse the count as you go up the opposite side completing 8 loops.

 # 25 Plate

You will also need to refer to Plate # 13 for reducing a bead. The two beads at the top and bottom of base strip.

Conchos

There seems to be a never ending parade of conchos being used today. They make for a southwestern look on whatever you attach them to; satin from China, lace from France, or leather from Texas. It's all cowboy when used with conchos.

These little metal disks have been done in silver by the Navajo Indian silversmiths for generations. My Navajo father "Ray Bedonie" in Flagstaff, Arizona is a silversmith and his ancestors before him. He makes beautiful silver concho belts.

The Mexican and South American people have a long history of wearing conchos. I have an ancient coin that looks like a concho. Many oriental coins take on the same shape. So who can really determine their origin?

In the making of saddles and headstalls, I have used leather conchos for fastening two pieces of leather tightly. I'm sure that method must date back to Rome, 100 B. C., for while in Italy, I saw a leather bags displayed from that period, conchos still in place.

Regardless of how the concho got its beginning, it's still has many uses today and we will illustrate some of its versatility in jewelry making for you.

Bead braiding, used with conchos, is a popular ornament technique. It's a wonderful craft for young people to enjoy. The boy scouts, girl scouts, Royal Ranger groups, and other young peoples organizations can use it creating items to be sold for fund raisers.

When working with beads that have large holes, it isn't always necessary to use a needle. Bead braiding is one of those instances. Crow beads are most commonly used for braiding. Younger people use the plastic beads for many reasons. They cost less then glass. They are available in almost any craft store and come in an array of shapes and colors. They don't break as easily as glass. As for me, I prefer the glass crow bead and I like to incorporate a few trade beads into the pattern.

Getting Started with Conchos and Bead Braiding

In plate #26, I have illustrated how to incorporate a concho with crow beads for a sew on to sweat shirts and other clothing. It's very easy to do.

For materials, you will need, #1-a heavy bead cord or leather lacing. The gold or silver lame' cord gives a look of shiny metal to the braid. # 2 beads with large holes. I suggest crow beads. # 3- key rings and conchos. The conchos can be any size as long as they have the two slits across for connections. (Some conchos are made solid) # 4-a tube of fabric or tacky glue.

Step 1--Cut two measures of cord or lacing, six times the length you want you finished piece to be. Using both cords as one. String a crow bead on and fold the cords in half, using the crow bed as center.

Step 2-From the back side of the concho weave all four ends of cord through the concho slits.

Step 3-Using both ends of one cord string the second crow bead on and snug lightly into place.

Step 4-Using the other cord, string both ends through the second crow bead. Notice in plate # 27 how each set of cords are brought around and on top of the last set of cords before passing through the crow bead.

Step 5-When you have braided on four crow beads, pass all four cord ends through a smaller bead. When you get the smaller bead in place, pull it back down just slightly and add a drop of glue. Then push the small bead back up over th glued spot. Adding the long bugles is optional. They are held on with a drop of glue to the top of the cord, then pushing the bugle bead over the glued spot.

Making a concho key chain is a quickie. Refer to plates 27 and 28.

Using leather for attaching conchos is easier than sewing on a button.

Step 1-Use a strip of leather about 1/2 inch wide and eight inches long. Find the center length of leather by folding in half. Mark center line with pencil on the inside of leather strip. That line will be next to the center bar on the concho.

Make a 1/4 inch slit in the leather 1/2 inch above the center line and another 1/2 inch below center line. (see plate # 30)

Pass the top end of leather lace through the bottom slit. Pull the top slit through the bottom slit. Next, pass the bottom end of lace through the unused slit and pull tight. This technique locks in place the concho and gives braided look to the lace. Carefully cut the ends of the leather lace into fringes and add a bead or glue a feather under and in with the bead for added ornament.

Bead Braided Necklaces

When using heart or tulip shaped beads, there is a simple beginning that strengthens the back of the necklace and avoids having to count the bead before you reverse the bead at center back.

To begin the necklace, cut four bead cords forty inches long. Fold two cords in half and tie a short length of string around one inch from the fold. Next, loop the other two cords through the first fold dividing the second set of cord in half at the fold. Refer to # 33 Plate.

Some people find it easier to just reverse the bead at the back of the necklace instead of looping the cords.

The loop helps to hold the right tension on the shorter braid, doing one side at a time.

When you have completed each side of the necklace, add a concho to the front and another bead to group the cords together. You may want to add a drop of glue to the cords before pushing the last bead into place.

Plate # 32 illustrated a button on

Button On Concho

concho with beads. The technique is simple and very quick. The button can be worn anywhere you can sew a button on.

The loop above the concho serves as a button hole and is the beginning of the project.

Thread two leather laces through a bead and center the bead. Next, pass all four ends under and over, then under the concho bar. Leave enough slack at the top for button hole loop and add at the top for button hole loop and add your three bead braid. The lace can be tied in on tie at the bottom or glued under the last bead. These little ornaments are great for attaching to boots or moccasins. You can also do a boot ankle bracelet with this bead braid and hang the concho on the side or toe of the boot.

Concho Beaded Earrings

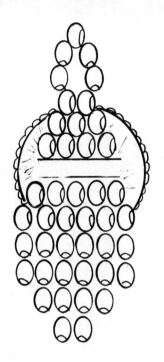

Brickstitch through Concho

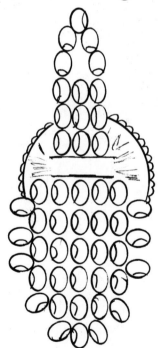

Off-Loom through Concho

Conchos and Bead Braiding

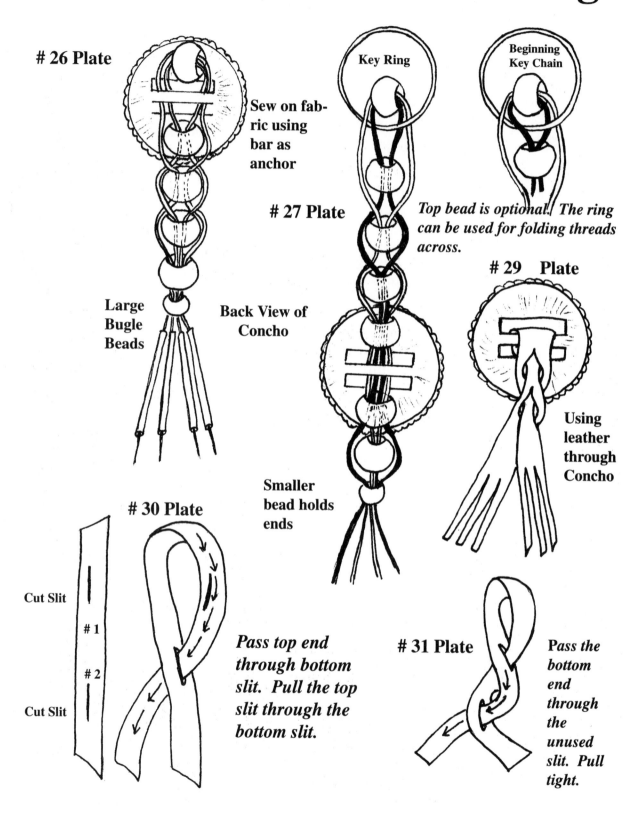

 # 26 Plate

Sew on fabric using bar as anchor

Large Bugle Beads

Key Ring

Beginning Key Chain

Top bead is optional. The ring can be used for folding threads across.

 # 27 Plate

Back View of Concho

Smaller bead holds ends

 # 29   Plate

Using leather through Concho

 # 30 Plate

Cut Slit

1

2

Cut Slit

Pass top end through bottom slit. Pull the top slit through the bottom slit.

 # 31 Plate

Pass the bottom end through the unused slit. Pull tight.

Bead Braided Necklace

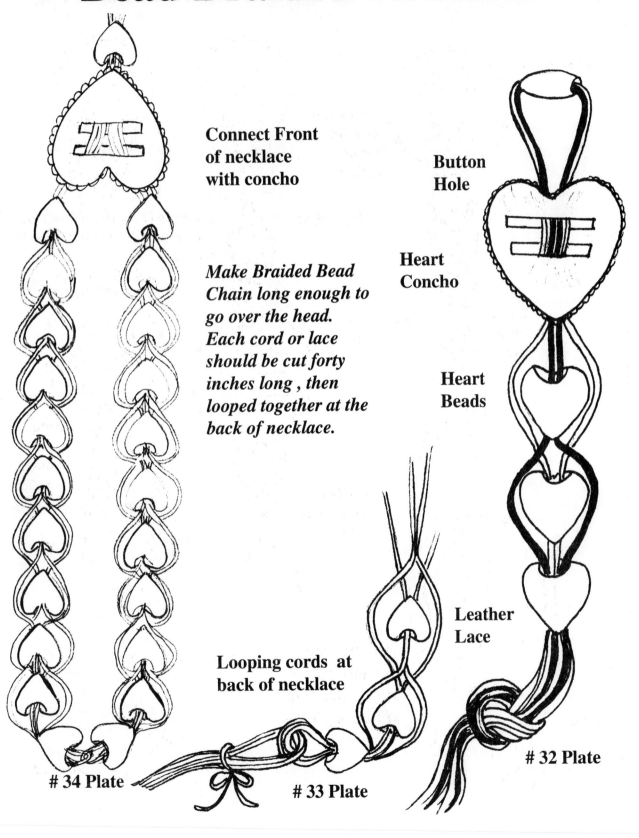

Connect Front of necklace with concho

Make Braided Bead Chain long enough to go over the head. Each cord or lace should be cut forty inches long , then looped together at the back of necklace.

Button Hole

Heart Concho

Heart Beads

Leather Lace

Looping cords at back of necklace

 # 34 Plate

 # 33 Plate

 # 32 Plate

ouble Needle Cross Over

The cross over technique can be done many ways and achieve a varied appearance each time. The basics can be incorporated with other weaves or used alone and still present a lovely elegant look.

The strength of the thread is very important when doing the necklace illustrated in plates # 35, # 36, and # 37. I prefer to use the Kevlar thread. It's very strong and almost impossible to break by pulling. The Kevlar thread is available in every basic color except white. So you have to choose your bead colors carefully. A darker thread will show through transparent beads and change the color. A size D Nymo thread will do for larger beads (size 10 seed). Adjust thread size according to bead size.

You will need a solid surface to fasten a cup hook or nail to. Next, thread two needles, one at each end of the same piece of thread about 1 1/2 yards long. Now you are ready to begin.

Step #1--loop one needle through the donut bead or jump ring. Then hang the donut bead onto the cup hook. Secure the thread position by passing both needles down through the first bead of the weave (see plate # 35). Pull the thread until half is equal to each needle.

Step #2--on needle #1 one pick up the two outside beads and center bead. Needle # 2, pick the two outside beads and pass # 2 needle horizontally, crossing the other thread through the center bead. Notice the needle positions and arrow movements illustrated in plate # 35. Repeat step # 2 using a progressively larger horizontal center bead as you go. When you have reached the center front of your necklace weave, begin reducing the horizontal center bead back to the original size of the first one.

To complete the neckline, pass both needles through the eye of a metal jewelry hook (see plate # 37). If possible, pass both needles down through the last bead again and tie a knot between the beads. If the bead is too small to go through again, then tie the knot between the hook and the last bead. Dab a tiny drop of clear nail polish on the knot.

Progressive fringe adds an elegant look to the necklace and is easy to do. See plate # 36 for illustrated instructions.

Earrings to match can also be made with cross needle technique. In the following pages are illustrated suggestions for earrings.

Double Needle Cross Over

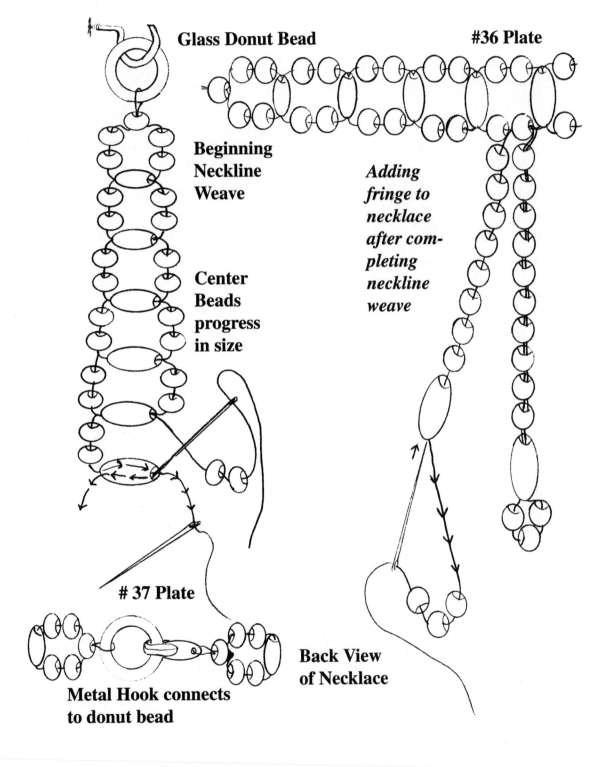

35 Plate

Glass Donut Bead

#36 Plate

Beginning
Neckline
Weave

*Adding
fringe to
necklace
after com-
pleting
neckline
weave*

Center
Beads
progress
in size

37 Plate

Metal Hook connects
to donut bead

Back View
of Necklace

Cross Needle Earrings

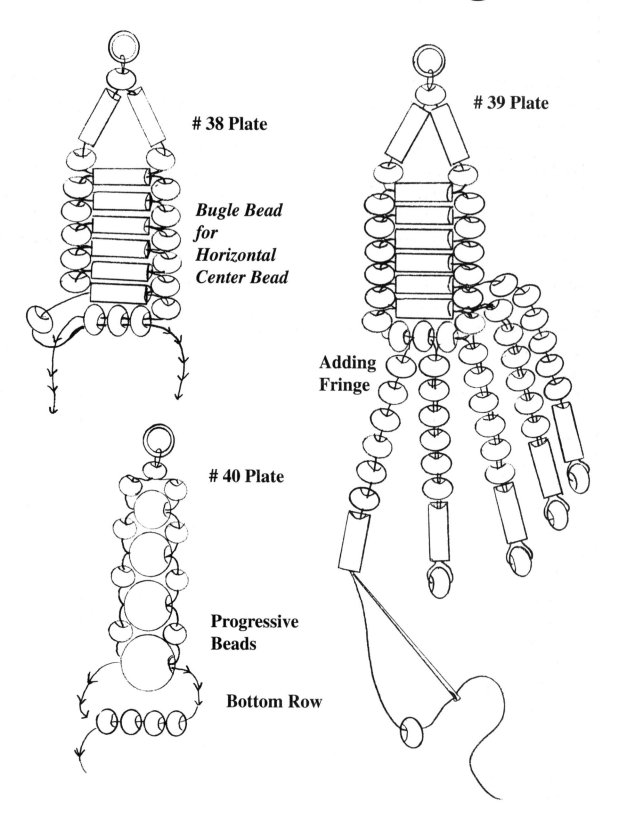

38 Plate

*Bugle Bead
for
Horizontal
Center Bead*

39 Plate

**Adding
Fringe**

40 Plate

**Progressive
Beads**

Bottom Row

ontemporary Bead Weaving

Contemporary is a wonderful way to use up your odd shaped beads in one project.

Any combination of colors and size beads you can fit in, makes for a slightly ethnic, contemporary effect.

Establishing a base to connect the odd beads to can be constructed many ways. Sometimes, a loomed strip is used. I have illustrated a chevron string for base row, combining the techniques already illustrated in Lacy Daisy with a turn bead chain of progressive numbered beads. Adding another off-loom weave of two rows, every fifth chevron.

There is an unlimited amount of designs to be accomplished just by using variations of beads as you fill in each chevron.

For step one--make a two bead off-loom weave as illustrated in plates # 16 and # 17.

Reduce row # 3--refer to plate # 20 illustration.

Attach a loop of beads to row # 3 for clasping necklace ends together at back.

Make a two bead off-loom weave at the other end of your chevron chain base. Connect a larger bead to be used as button through loop (see plate # 43).

Step 2--As you string your base row of beads, place a turn bead every tenth bead and progress your chevron base row to a larger chevron by adding two beads before each turn bead.

Weave a double row of "off-loom beads" periodically as your base progresses. It adds a little more stability and gives a more perplexing look.

I realize how difficult this technique sounds, but if you give it a try, I'm sure you will enjoy the outcome. It's amazing how beading transforms your confidence when you complete a project. It's fun to say, " I can do that" and show off your work.

For a real show stopper; try the base rows illustrated in "Cross Needle Earrings, Plates # 38 and # 39". Attach a multiple amount of left over beads in varied fringe lengths (longer fringes to the front of necklace). An amazing transaction takes form. One, I'm sure you'll be proud to wear.

The following illustrations are just one example on contemporary beading. Experiment with your own ideas and create a masterpiece.

Contemporary Bead Weaving

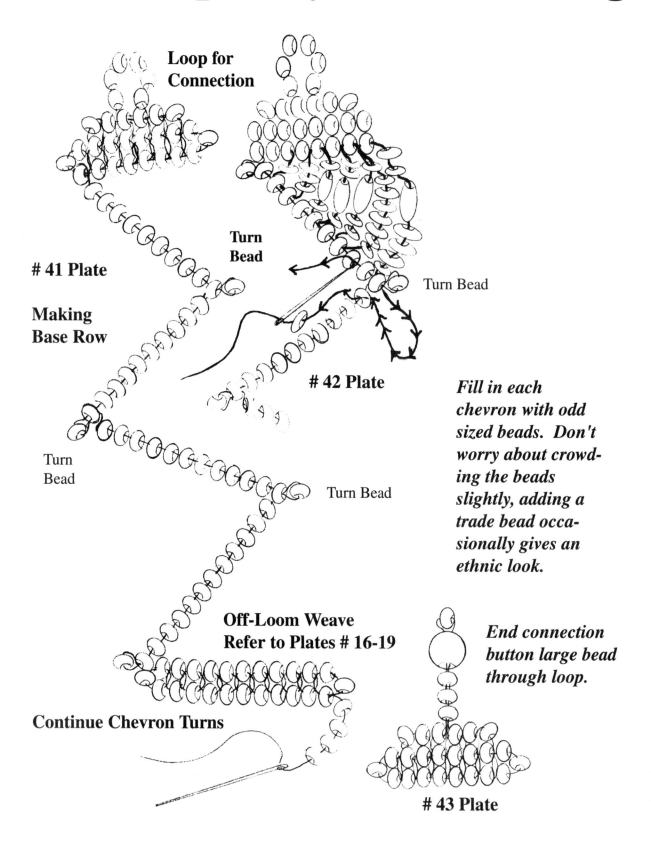

Loop for Connection

Turn Bead

 # 41 Plate

Making Base Row

Turn Bead

Turn Bead

 # 42 Plate

Turn Bead

Fill in each chevron with odd sized beads. Don't worry about crowding the beads slightly, adding a trade bead occasionally gives an ethnic look.

Off-Loom Weave Refer to Plates # 16-19

Continue Chevron Turns

End connection button large bead through loop.

 # 43 Plate

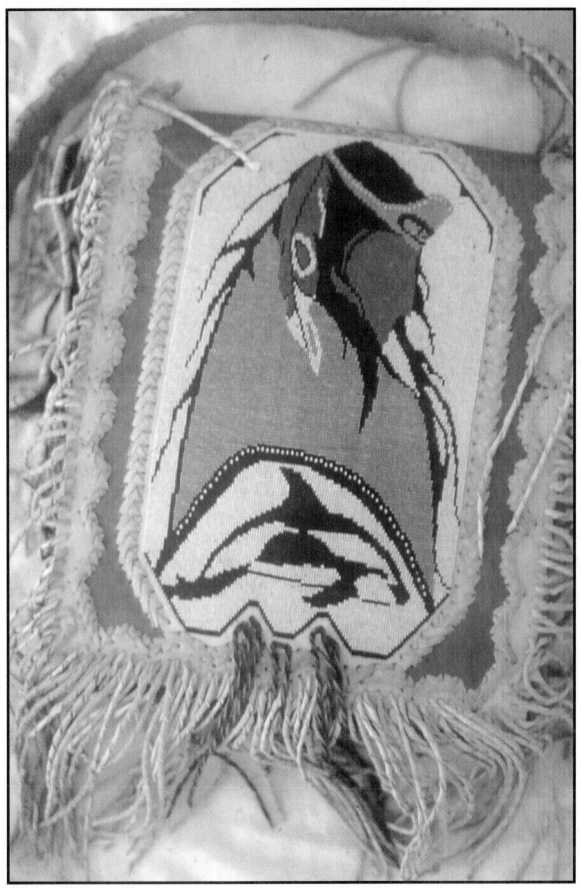

Melody Abbott continues to amaze us with her beautiful Beaded Loom Weaving and creative pattern designs. This purse is also shown in the color section.

Beaded Boot Spats

In Volume 5, we show a pair of white cowboy boots with beadwork covering the toe and up the front. These beaded spats can be transferred to any western boot with a heel.

The spats shown in Volume 5 were done in an off-loom weave illustrated in Volume 3. The beadwork was glued in place on soft beading leather, then hand sewed along all outside edges. The beaded spats are connected to the boot in four places. First, around the top of the boot with a leather strap passing through the boot pulls on each side, then the strap snaps together. The second strap goes around the ankle and snaps together. The third strap goes under the boot and next to the heel. This strap is leather with a two inch piece of heavy duty elastic in the middle, then leather. The boot toe is slipped through this undersling strap and the elastic part worn next to the heel. (no snap)

The fourth connection is "velcro". Velcro is a wonderful invention for taking the place of snaps, zippers and sewing on buttons. It comes in little round, self-adhesive, disks that can be placed on almost any surface with great, wearable results. The toe area of beadwork is held on with velcro disks-- arranged in a triangle on the toe with one center.

These boot spats are for show, not rough riding. They hold well for western swing and boot scootin' dancing. But not for horseback! I'm afraid they are limited to parades only.

Other than doing the beadwork, the following illustrations are self-explanatory.

I do need to emphasize the importance of reversing the "leather backing pattern". Otherwise, one of your spats will snap on the outside of your leg. Use only heavy duty snaps. This technique also works with moccasins. And with a slight alteration, can be worn on jacket sleeves.

The bear pattern used for the beadwork on the western boots shown in Volume 5, is graphed on page 54 of Volume 4. The bear paw is in graph on the front cover of Volume 6.

When adding the bead fringes, make sure they are not too long around the toe area. If they drag the ground, your beadwork won't last.

Beaded Boot Spats

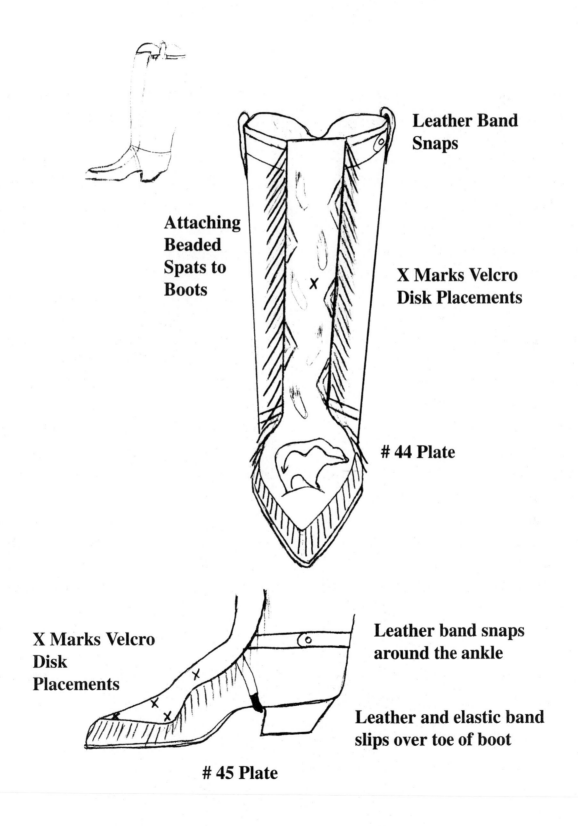

Leather Band Snaps

Attaching Beaded Spats to Boots

X Marks Velcro Disk Placements

 # 44 Plate

X Marks Velcro Disk Placements

Leather band snaps around the ankle

Leather and elastic band slips over toe of boot

 # 45 Plate

Leather Backing for Beaded Boot Spats

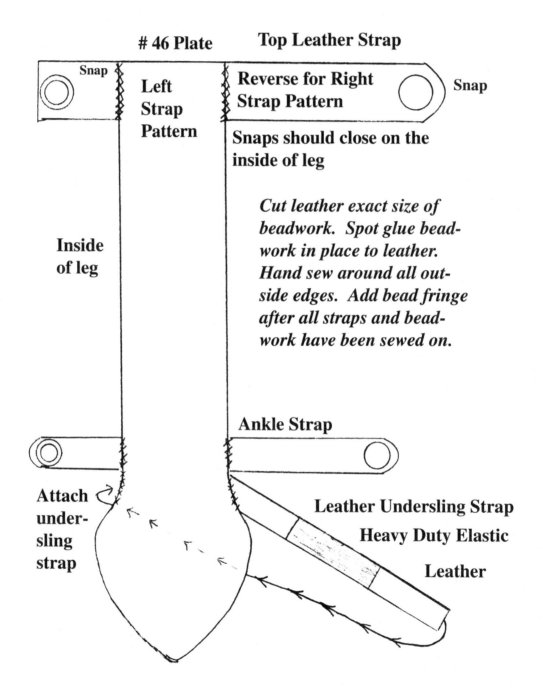

46 Plate

Top Leather Strap

Snap

Left Strap Pattern

Reverse for Right Strap Pattern

Snap

Snaps should close on the inside of leg

Cut leather exact size of beadwork. Spot glue beadwork in place to leather. Hand sew around all outside edges. Add bead fringe after all straps and beadwork have been sewed on.

Inside of leg

Ankle Strap

Attach undersling strap

Leather Undersling Strap

Heavy Duty Elastic

Leather

BEADS TO BUCKSKINS

Glossary of Bead Phrasing

1. **Bar Pin**--an attachment for pinning onto a garment with blank front for attaching beadwork or glue on other ornaments.
2. **Bead Shovel**--tiny scoop shovel used for small beads.
3. **Bead Tip Cement**--glue used in beadwork.
4. **Big Eye Needle**--special needle that sews from both ends and springs open in the middle for threading.
5. **Button Cover**--metal cover that slips over button and clips in place with blank front for attaching beads or stones.
6. **Cabochons**--a smooth stone, usually flat on the bottom side and raised, quarter moon shaped on the top side.
7. **Concho**--metal disk with two large slits centered for connecting with leather or heavy cord.
8. **Cut Beads**--beads that have been faceted on one or more sides for sparkle.
9. **Czech Beads**--beads made in Czechoslovakia.
10. **Druks**--smooth, rounded glass beads.
11. **Earring Drops**--(metal) flat disks, usually filigree in assorted sizes and shapes
12. **Earring Findings**--ear past; flat, metal disk with steel post which connects through pierced ear with a metal ear back. French hook--metal wire shaped (for pierced ears) similar to fish hook which has a loop on the front side for hooking beadwork on. Kidney Ear wire--pierced earring wire shaped like a kidney and closes as a safety pin. Ear clip--earring base for non-pierced ears. Rounded hoops--with a metal loop for attaching ear wire or drop bead in center. Used for hoop beaded earrings or dream catcher earrings; comes also in teardrop shapes of assorted sizes.
13. **Filigree Beads**--ornated metal beads in assorted shapes and sizes.
14. **Fire Polish Beads**--beads that have a fired finish that gives a shinning iridescent look.
15. **Fresh Water Pearls**--an inexpensive pearl, usually rice shaped in assorted sizes.
16. **Glass Bugle Beads**--Beads made in tube shape. Available in millimeter measured length sizes.

17. **Hex Beads**--hexagon shaped beads.

18. **Heishi**--beads made of shell.

19. **Knot Bead**--seed bead tied with one tie that serves as a knot to hold first beads of the project in place. The knot bead is to be removed and thread end worked into finished beadwork.

20. **Liquid Silver**--silver plated liquid silver beads, shaped like tubes (bugle beads). Sometimes twisted or hot dog.

21. **Loom**--devise used for loomed bead weaving.

22. **Metallic Beads**--bead that gives the appearance of metal or is constructed of metal and other elements.

23. **Nymo Beading Thread**--a very fine strong nylon thread designed to be used with seed beads and comes in sizes (small to large) 000-00-0-A-B-C-D. Kevlar--a super strong beading thread, used to make bullet-proof vests, etc.

24. **Rondelles**--flat shaped beads.

25. **Rosette**--round object; as in beadwork "Beaded Rosette

26. **Seed Beads**--on needle measurements, the larger the number, the smaller the bead or needle.

27. **Some abbreviated catalog color descriptions of beads:**

OP-Opaque	DY-Dyed
IR-Iris	SL-Silver-lined
MET-Metallic	TR-Transparent

Example: 500 g. Bugles--TR-IR-Aqua #2

Translation: 500 grams of bugle beads, transparent and Iris Aqua in Size #2.

28. **Stone Beads**--usually made of semi-precious stones such as amethyst, garnet, malachite, citrine, topaz, adventurine, quartz, jasper, obsidian, mother of pearl, sodalite, carnelian, onyx, blue lace and other agates. Cabochons are also made of these stones in assorted sizes.

29. **Tambour Needle**--a set of three different size needles with a small hook for a point. Each set has one handle with an insert turn screw that adjusts to hold needle tight when inserted.

30. **Tiger Tail**--nylon coated cable for stringing necklaces or bracelets.

31. **Turn Bead**--the bead used at the end of a fringe.